The Key to Solving High-Conflict Divorce in the Family Courts:

Proposal for a Pilot Program in the Family Law Courts

C.A. Childress, Psy.D.

Oaksong Press

The Key to Solving High-Conflict Divorce in the Family Courts: Proposal for a Pilot Program in the Family Law Courts

Oaksong Press, Claremont, California

Printed in the United States of America

ISBN: 978-0-9961145-6-1

Table of Contents

THE CHILDRESS INSTITUTE • 219 N. INDIAN HILL BLVD., STE 201 • CLAREMONT, CA 91711

THE CHILDRESS INSTITUTE: Mission Statement

To use the latest scientific knowledge in the fields of child development and the healthy neuro-development of the brain during childhood to create solutions for the social, emotional, and psychological challenges facing children and their families.

CURRENT FOCUS: Parental Alienation in High-Conflict Divorce

Creating the solution to the family pathology of "parental alienation" in high-conflict divorce by providing training and Certification to mental health and legal professionals in an attachment-based model of "parental alienation" (AB-PA). An attachment-based model of the family pathology traditionally called "parental alienation" defines the pathology from entirely within standard and established constructs and principles of professional psychology.

Future Projects & Directions of THE CHILDRESS INSTITUTE

The Terrorist Mind: Developing an attachment-based understanding of the terrorist mind, pathological hatred, and fanatical extremism, with the goal of developing primary and secondary treatment-related interventions to resolve the social and psychological trauma-related pathology of terrorism and the extremism of pathological anger.

Developmentally Supportive Parenting, ADHD, & Foster Parenting: Providing education and training in developmentally supportive parenting for all parents and all families, with a special focus on providing education and training in relationship-based parenting that can effectively resolve the symptoms of attention deficits, impulsivity, and hyperactive behavior in children through non-medication relationship-based parenting approaches, and training in developmentally supportive parenting for foster parents.

Redeveloping Education Infrastructure: Providing leadership in developing a model for foundationally reformulating the educational approach for children in the United States away from the current 12th Century "Cathedral School" model toward a 22nd Century education model based in the scientific research on child development, the scientific research on learning, and the current advances in the full range of available information technology and media.

Reduction of Prison Recidivism: Intervention-development and research into catalytic intervention models for reducing the trauma-impacted mindset that leads to recidivism in released prisoners and juvenile offenders.

THE CHILDRESS INSTITUTE: *Internationale*

The Childress Institute Internationale will be an over-seas extension of the vision and mission of the Childress Institute.

International Extension of The Childress Institute

The Terrorist Mind & the Extremism of Pathological Anger:

This future division of The Childress Institute Internationale represents an extension of the U.S. Terrorist Mind and Pathological Anger division of The Childress Institute into the European and South-East Asian regions, examining the attachment-trauma origins of the terrorist mind and the extremism of pathological anger in these socio-cultural contexts.

The Socio-Trauma and Attachment-Related Trauma Origins of International Conflict:

This future division of The Childress Institute Internationale will consist of two components:

1.) Trauma Origins of International Conflict: An examination of the origins of international conflict in the history of socio-cultural and attachment-related trauma.

2.) Trauma-Focused Resolution of International Conflict: The resolution of the propensity for and risk of inter-ethnic and inter-nation conflict through socio-psychological *Development* intervention responses to the socio-historical psychological trauma that are aimed at resolving the socio-psychological sequelae of attachment-related trauma (as identified in the Origins Component of the project).

The Key to Solving High-Conflict Divorce in the Family Courts: Proposal for a Pilot Program in the Family Law Courts

Background

High-conflict divorce disproportionately congests the family law system with continual litigation and is intractable to mental health therapy. Various mental health efforts have been tried in the past to limit and control the family conflict that leads to endless litigation, such as family mediation to resolve disputes outside of the court system, or child custody evaluations to provide formal mental health recommendations into the court's custody related decisions. However, these efforts toward solution have had only limited success as evidenced by unsolved family conflicts and the continuing burden placed on the family court system by high-conflict divorce cases.

Resolving parents' continual conflict over child custody can be one of the most challenging decisions for the court system, and can entangle the child into the inter-spousal conflict of the parents by making the child a "custody prize" to be won in their inter-spousal conflict. This can lead to covert and sometimes overt psychological pressure being placed on the child by one parent to create the child's rejection of the other parent following divorce, a process that has received the label of "parental alienation" in the popular culture.

Children have the right of childhood to love both parents and to receive the love of both parents in return. Child custody is not a prize to be won by the "better parent" as a symbol of parental (spousal) superiority, and children should never become weapons to be used by one parent to inflict suffering on the other spouse-and-parent surrounding the divorce. Using psychological pressure and manipulative techniques of psychological control (Barber, 2002)[1] in order to manipulate the child's thoughts and feelings so as to undermine the child's love and attachment to the other parent is reprehensible parenting that severely damages the child's emotional and psychological development.

Parental Alienation: Changing Paradigm

The attachment-related family pathology of "parental alienation" has come to be defined in the popular culture as the child rejecting a relationship with one parent (the targeted parent) as a consequence of negative parental influence applied to the child by the other parent (the allied and supposedly "favored" parent). The term "parental alienation" was popularized in the mid-1980s by a psychiatrist, Richard Gardner, who proposed a new form of pathology in mental health called *Parental Alienation Syndrome* (PAS) that was supposedly identifiable by a unique new set of symptom identifiers that Gardner made up based solely on his clinical experience. Gardner also proposed that this supposedly new form of pathology (in which one parent manipulated the child to create the child's rejection of the other parent) was often associated with false allegations of child abuse made by mothers against fathers.

Gardner's proposal for a new form of pathology (a "new syndrome") that was unique in all of mental health generated considerable controversy in professional psychology. The controversy created by Gardner's supposedly "new form of pathology" led to a schism within the field of professional psychology between

---

[1] Barber, B. K. (Ed.) (2002). Intrusive parenting: How psychological control affects children and adolescents. Washington, DC: American Psychological Association.

adherents and opponents of the PAS model. This schism in professional psychology created by a Gardnerian PAS definition of the pathology undermines the professional mental health response to this day, leading to inaccurate assessments, imprecise diagnosis, and ineffective treatment.

In proposing a "new syndrome" – a new form of pathology - that was unique in all of professional psychology, Gardner led everyone off of the path of professionally established constructs and principles and into the wilderness of supposedly new forms of pathology. The solution to the attachment-related family pathology traditionally called "parental alienation" surrounding high-conflict divorce is to be found in leaving the realm of supposedly "new forms of pathology" and returning to the professionally established constructs and principles of professional psychology. Returning to standard and established constructs and principles of professional psychology leads to appropriate assessment, accurate diagnosis, and effective treatment for all forms of pathology, including the attachment-related family pathology traditionally called "parental alienation."

Attachment-Based "Parental Alienation" (AB-PA)

An attachment-based model of "parental alienation" (*Foundations*: Childress, 2015)[2] defines the attachment-related family pathology traditionally called "parental alienation" in the popular culture from entirely within standard and established constructs and principles of professional psychology (the attachment system; personality disorder pathology; family systems constructs). This leads directly to assessment models that accurately diagnosis the pathology when it is present, and that also accurately diagnose when it is not present.

By returning to standard and established constructs and principles of professional psychology, AB-PA identifies four domains of professional knowledge required for professional competence in assessment, diagnosis, and treatment:

> **The Attachment System:** A professional-level knowledge and expertise is required regarding the attachment system, what it is, how it functions, and how it characteristically dysfunctions; including issues of grief surrounding loss, the formation and role of internal working models of attachment (attachment schemas), and the transmission of attachment trauma across generations.
>
> **Personality Disorder Pathology:** A professional-level knowledge and expertise is required regarding narcissistic and borderline personality pathology, the origins of these types of personality pathology within childhood attachment trauma, the assessment and diagnosis of narcissistic and borderline personality traits, and the characteristic expression of narcissistic and borderline personality pathology within family relationships, including role-reversal parent-child relationships, use of the child as a "regulatory object" to stabilize the parent's pathology, and the collapse of the narcissistic and borderline personality structure in response to divorce.
>
> **Family Systems Therapy:** A professional-level knowledge is required for family systems constructs, including homeostasis, triangulation, cross-generational coalitions, and emotional cutoffs, and regarding the principles of family systems therapy to restore normal-range and healthy family relationships.
>
> **Complex Trauma:** Complex trauma is the chronic exposure to relationship-based emotionally and psychologically traumatic experiences. A professional-level of knowledge and expertise is required in recognizing and diagnosing the impact of complex trauma, the trans-generational transmission of complex trauma in reenactment narratives, and the differential symptoms of authentic current trauma versus trauma reenactment.

[2] Childress, C.A. (2015). An attachment-based model of parental alienation: Foundations. Claremont, CA: Oaksong Press.

An Attachment-Related Pathology

The attachment system is the brain system that governs all aspects of love and bonding across the lifespan, including grief and loss. The attachment system is the brain system responsible for motivating children's affectional bond to parents. A child rejecting a parent is fundamentally an attachment-related pathology.

The premier researcher in the attachment system, Mary Ainsworth, describes the attachment system,

> "I define an "affectional bond" as a relatively long-enduring tie in which the partner is important as a unique individual and is interchangeable with none other. In an affectional bond, there is a desire to maintain closeness to the partner. In older children and adults, that closeness may to some extent be sustained over time and distance and during absences, but nevertheless there is at least an intermittent desire to reestablish proximity and interaction, and pleasure – often joy – upon reunion. Inexplicable separation tends to cause distress, and permanent loss would cause grief."

> "An 'attachment' is an affectional bond, and hence an attachment figure is never wholly interchangeable with or replaceable by another, even though there may be others to whom one is also attached. In attachments, as in other affectional bonds, there is a need to maintain proximity, distress upon inexplicable separation, pleasure and joy upon reunion, and grief at loss." (Ainsworth, 1989, p. 711)[3]

The attachment system was first described by John Bowlby in a set of three volumes describing the formation of attachment bonds (1969),[4] the response to separation (1973),[5] and grief at loss (1980).[6] Bowlby identified that the deactivation of attachment bonding is caused by the "pathological mourning" of loss;

> "The deactivation of attachment behavior is a key feature of certain common variants of pathological mourning." (Bowlby, 1980, p. 70)

Bowlby further identified the process of disordered mourning as the expression of personality pathology created through adverse childhood relationship experiences,

> "Disturbances of personality, which include a bias to respond to loss with disordered mourning, are seen as the outcome of one or more deviations in development that can originate or grow worse during any of the years of infancy, childhood and adolescence." (Bowlby, 1980, p. 217)

The advantage of returning to standard and established constructs and principles of professional psychology is clear. Once we return to standard and established constructs, the pathology of a child rejecting a parent is immediately identified as an attachment-related pathology of "pathological mourning" that is associated with personality pathology within the family.

Turning then to the field of personality disorder pathology, one of the leading figures in describing narcissistic and borderline personality pathology, Otto Kernberg, identifies that the pathological processing of sadness and "mournful longing" is a basic feature of the narcissistic and borderline personality disorder structure;

> "They are especially deficient in genuine feelings of sadness and mournful longing; their incapacity for experiencing depressive reactions is a basic feature of their personalities. When abandoned or disappointed by other people they may show what on the surface looks like depression, but which on

---

[3] Ainsworth, M.D.S. (1989). Attachments beyond infancy. American Psychologist, 44, 709-716.

[4] Bowlby, J. (1969). Attachment and loss. Vol. 1. Attachment. NY: Basic Books.

[5] Bowlby, J. (1973). Attachment and loss: Vol. 2. Separation: Anxiety and anger. NY: Basic Books.

[6] Bowlby, J. (1980). Attachment and loss: Vol. 3. Loss: Sadness and depression. NY: Basic Books.

further examination emerges as anger and resentment, loaded with revengeful wishes, rather than real sadness for the loss of a person whom they appreciated." (Kernberg, 1975, p. 229)[7]

In the attachment-related family pathology traditionally called "parental alienation" in the popular culture, the allied parent is the primary case of "pathological mourning" surrounding the loss of the *spousal* attachment bond through the divorce. The natural "sadness and mournful longing" of this parent is then being translated by this parent's personality pathology into "anger and resentment, loaded with revengeful wishes" toward the other *spouse*/(parent) in the divorce. The "disordered mourning" of the allied narcissistic/(borderline) personality parent is then being transferred to the child through the **manipulation** and **psychological control** exercised on the child by the allied narcissistic parent through the formation of a "cross-generational coalition" with the child against the other parent.

Family Systems Pathology

Divorce ends the marriage, but not the family. With divorce, the family structure transitions from an ***intact family structure*** that was previously united by the marriage, to a new ***separated family structure*** that is now united by the children through the parents' continuing co-parenting responsibilities and by the continuing bonds of shared affection between the children and both parents.

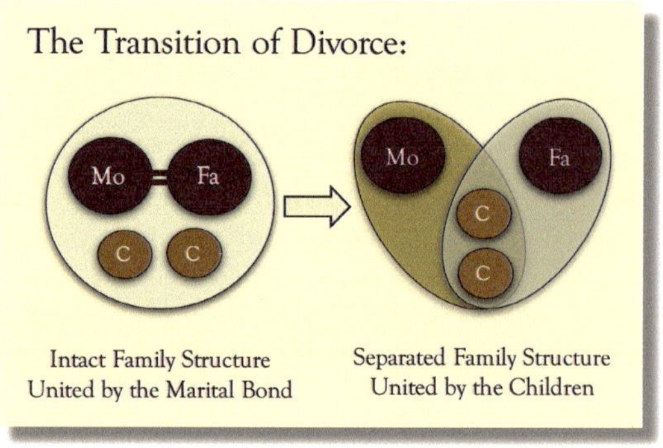

Families must adapt to various transitions over the developmental course of the family. A central tenet of family systems therapy is that when a family is unable to successfully adapt to a transition, symptoms emerge within the family (often with the children) to stabilize the family's maladaptive functioning. Divorce represents one of the most impactful transitions that any family must navigate; the transition from an intact family structure united by the marriage to a new post-divorce separated family structure that is now being united by the shared bonds of affection between the parents and children.

When a family cannot adaptively respond to a transition, "triangles" develop in family relationships in which the two-person spousal conflict is expanded into a three-personal ***parent-child-parent*** conflict. In maladaptive families, the child is drawn into the inter-spousal conflict ("triangulated") by one or both parents to stabilize the family's functioning. Triangulating the child into the spousal conflict is often through the formation of a "***cross-generational coalition***" of the child with one parent against the other parent. The preeminent family systems therapist, Jay Haley, provides a definition of the family pathology of a cross-generational coalition of one parent with the child against the other parent:

> "The people responding to each other in the triangle are not peers, but one of them is of a different generation from the other two... In the process of their interaction together, the person of one generation forms a coalition with the person of the other generation against his peer. By 'coalition' is meant a process of joint action which is *against* the third person... The coalition between the two persons is denied. That is, there is certain behavior which indicates a coalition which, when it is queried, will be denied as a coalition... In essence, the perverse triangle is one in which the separation of generations is

[7] Kernberg, O.F. (1975). Borderline conditions and pathological narcissism. New York: Aronson.

breached in a covert way. When this occurs as a repetitive pattern, the system will be pathological." (Haley, 1977, p. 37)[8]

Haley calls this form of family pathology "perverse" because the cross-generational coalition violates generational boundaries between the child and parent. In the *Journal of Emotional Abuse*, Kerig describes the severity of "boundary dissolutions" in which the psychological autonomy of the child is violated,

> "The breakdown of appropriate generational boundaries between parents and children significantly increases the risk for emotional abuse... When parent-child boundaries are violated, the implications for developmental psychopathology are significant. Poor boundaries interfere with the child's capacity to progress through development which, as Anna Freud (1965) suggested, is the defining feature of childhood psychopathology." (Kerig, 2005, p. 6-7)

In extreme cases of a cross-generational coalition involving an alliance of the child with a narcissistic and/or borderline personality parent, the child's alliance to the narcissistic or borderline personality parent can require that the child entirely rejects a relationship with the other parent, the targeted parent. One of the principle founders of family systems therapy, Murray Bowen, refers to the symptom of one family member rejecting another family member as an "emotional cutoff" (Bowen, 1978; Titelman, 2003).[9] The pathology traditionally called "parental alienation" in the popular culture represents the symptomatic expression by the child of an ***emotional cutoff*** of the child from a parent as a result of the family's unsuccessful transition to a functional separated family structure that is now united by the shared bonds of affection between the child with both parents.

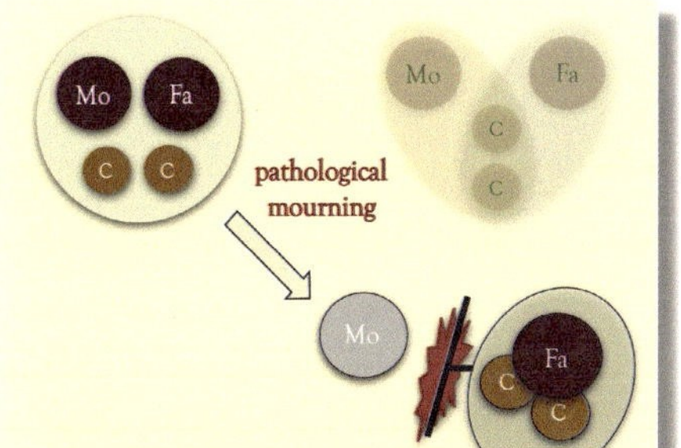

The cutoff family structure of "parental alienation

The family's inability to transition to a healthy separated family structure is being caused by the narcissistic parent's inability to process this parent's own sadness and grief surrounding the divorce. This narcissistic or borderline personality parent is instead translating his or her own sadness, grief, and loss into "anger and resentment, loaded with revengeful wishes" toward the other spouse, and this parent is then forming a ***cross-generational coalition*** with the child against the other spouse-as-a-parent as a means of stabilizing this parent's own personality pathology. The narcissistic/(borderline) personality parent is transferring his or her own "disordered mourning," anger, and resentment toward the other ***spouse*** to the child through aberrant and distorted parenting practices of psychological control and psychological manipulation.

On page 42 of their book *Family Healing* (1993),[10] the preeminent family systems therapist Salvador Minuchin and his co-author Michael Nichols provide a structural diagram of the *cross-generational coalition* of a father and child, and the *cutoff* in the relationship with the mother created by this cross-generational coalition in the family. This diagram depicts the child's *triangulation* into the spousal conflict (the triangular pattern in the family's relationships) through the formation of a cross-generational coalition of the child with the father against the mother. The cross-generational coalition of the child with the father elevates the child in the family hierarchy to a position above that of the mother (an "inverted hierarchy"), from which the child then feels entitled to judge

[8] Haley, J. (1977). Toward a theory of pathological systems. In P. Watzlawick & J. Weakland (Eds.), The interactional view (pp. 31-48). New York: Norton.

[9] Bowen, M. (1978). Family Therapy in Clinical Practice. New York: Jason Aronson.

Titelman, P. (2003). Emotional cutoff in Bowen family systems theory: An Overview. In Emotional cutoff: Bowen family systems theory perspectives, P. Titelman (ed). New York: Haworth Press.

[10] Minuchin. S. & Nichols, M.P. (1993). Family healing: Strategies for hope and understanding. New York: Touchstone.

the adequacy of the mother as a parent and as a person, supported by the empowering coalition with the father. The three lines between the father and child indicate a psychologically "enmeshed" relationship involving a fusion of psychological perception which represents a psychological boundary violation of the child's independent autonomy.

Minuchin. S. & Nichols, M.P. (1993). Family healing: Strategies for hope and understanding. New York: Touchstone.

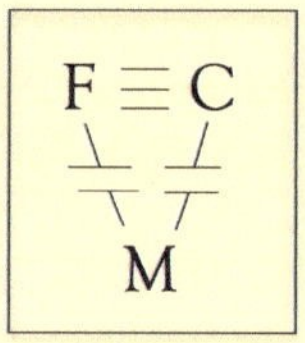

Inverted Hierarchy, Enmeshment, Cross-Generational Coalition, & Cutoff of Mother

(Minuchin & Nichols, p. 42)

An attachment-based model of "parental alienation" (AB-PA) is not proposing a new form of pathology, but is instead applying the standard and established constructs and principles of professional psychology to a set of symptoms. In professional psychology, the application of standard and established constructs and principles to a set of symptoms is called diagnosis. An attachment-based model of "parental alienation" returns us to the established path of professional psychology by diagnosing the pathology from entirely within standard and established constructs and principles of professional psychology.

Psychological Control of the Child

The manipulative psychological control of the child by a parent is a scientifically established family relationship pattern in dysfunctional family systems. In his book regarding parental psychological control of children, *Intrusive Parenting: How Psychological Control Affects Children and Adolescents,*[11] published by the American Psychological Association, Brian Barber and his colleague, Elizabeth Harmon, identify over 30 empirically validated scientific studies that have established the construct of parental psychological control of children.

Barber and Harmon offer the following definition for the construct of parental psychological control of the child:

> "Psychological control refers to parental behaviors that are intrusive and manipulative of children's thoughts, feelings, and attachment to parents. These behaviors appear to be associated with disturbances in the psychoemotional boundaries between the child and parent, and hence with the development of an independent sense of self and identity." (Barber & Harmon, 2002, p. 15)[12]

According to Stone, Bueler, and Barber:

> "The central elements of psychological control are intrusion into the child's psychological world and self-definition and parental attempts to manipulate the child's thoughts and feelings through invoking guilt, shame, and anxiety. Psychological control is distinguished from behavioral control in that the parent attempts to control, through the use of criticism, dominance, and anxiety or guilt induction, the youth's thoughts and feelings rather than the youth's behavior." (Stone, Buehler, & Barber, 2002, p. 57)[13]

Soenens and Vansteenkiste (2010) describe the various methods used to achieve parental psychological control of the child:

---

[11] Barber, B. K. (Ed.) (2002). Intrusive parenting: How psychological control affects children and adolescents. Washington, DC: American Psychological Association.

[12] Barber, B. K. and Harmon, E. L. (2002). Violating the self: Parenting psychological control of children and adolescents. In B. K. Barber (Ed.), Intrusive parenting (pp. 15-52). Washington, DC: American Psychological Association.

[13] Stone, G., Buehler, C., & Barber, B. K. (2002) Interparental conflict, parental psychological control, and youth problem behaviors. In B. K. Barber (Ed.), Intrusive parenting: How psychological control affects children and adolescents. Washington, DC: American Psychological Association.

"Psychological control can be expressed through a variety of parental tactics, including (a) guilt-induction, which refers to the use of guilt inducing strategies to pressure children to comply with a parental request; (b) contingent love or love withdrawal, where parents make their attention, interest, care, and love contingent upon the children's attainment of parental standards; (c) instilling anxiety, which refers to the induction of anxiety to make children comply with parental requests; and (d) invalidation of the child's perspective, which pertains to parental constraining of the child's spontaneous expression of thoughts and feelings." (Soenens & Vansteenkiste, 2010, p. 75)[14]

Research by Stone, Buehler, and Barber establishes the link between parental psychological control of children and marital conflict:

"This study was conducted using two different samples of youth. The first sample consisted of youth living in Knox County, Tennessee. The second sample consisted of youth living in Ogden, Utah." (Stone, Buehler, & Barber, 2002, p. 62)

"The analyses reveal that variability in psychological control used by parents is not random but it is linked to interparental conflict, particularly covert conflict. Higher levels of covert conflict in the marital relationship heighten the likelihood that parents would use psychological control with their children." (Stone, Buehler, & Barber, 2002, p. 86)

Stone, Buehler, and Barber offer an explanation for their finding that intrusive parental psychological control of children is related to high inter-spousal conflict:

"The concept of triangles 'describes the way any three people relate to each other and involve others in emotional issues between them' (Bowen, 1989, p. 306). In the anxiety-filled environment of conflict, a third person is triangulated, either temporarily or permanently, to ease the anxious feelings of the conflicting partners. By default, that third person is exposed to an anxiety-provoking and disturbing atmosphere. For example, a child might become the scapegoat or focus of attention, thereby transferring the tension from the marital dyad to the parent-child dyad. Unresolved tension in the marital relationship might spill over to the parent-child relationship through parents' use of psychological control as a way of securing and maintaining a strong emotional alliance and level of support from the child. As a consequence, the triangulated youth might feel pressured or obliged to listen to or agree with one parents' complaints against the other. The resulting enmeshment and cross-generational coalition would exemplify parents' use of psychological control to coerce and maintain a parent-youth emotional alliance against the other parent (Haley, 1976; Minuchin, 1974)." (Stone, Buehler, & Barber, 2002, p. 86-87)

Foundations

We begin constructing any structure, including the solution to high-conflict divorce within the family law system, by laying a solid foundation for the structure we are to build. *An Attachment-Based Model of Parental Alienation: Foundations* (Childress, 2015),[15] lays this solid foundation for the resolution of high-conflict divorce by fully defining the pathology traditionally called "parental alienation" from entirely within standard and established constructs and principles of professional psychology. By returning to established standards of practice for professional psychology, an attachment-based model of "parental alienation" (AB-PA) provides the *Foundations* for the solution. It leads directly to a structured protocol for professional assessment and to a set of three definitive diagnostic indicators of the pathology.

[14] Soenens, B., & Vansteenkiste, M. (2010). A theoretical upgrade of the concept of parental psychological control: Proposing new insights on the basis of self-determination theory. Developmental Review, 30, 74–99.
[15] Childress, C.A. (2015). An attachment-based model of parental alienation: Foundations. Claremont, CA: Oaksong Press.

Pilot Program Proposal for the Family Court System

The Key Solution for High-Conflict Divorce

Creating the solution to the family pathology of "parental alienation" in high-conflict divorce requires specialized professional knowledge and expertise from mental health that can effectively resolve the pathology and that can effectively collaborate with the Court in reducing the litigation surrounding family conflict.

THE CHILDRESS INSTITUTE is proposing a family law pilot program to provide the Court with the needed professional expertise to effectively resolve and manage the family pathology creating high-conflict divorce.

The Key to solving the attachment-related family pathology of "parental alienation" in high-conflict divorce involves creating a mental health and legal team with the required professional expertise to actively take charge in solving the family pathology surrounding high-conflict divorce. The Key to unlocking high-conflict divorce is the teaming of an AB-PA Certified mental health professional who has the required professional expertise to solve the family conflict surrounding the attachment-related pathology of AB-PA, with an AB-PA Knowledgeable amicus attorney who can work collaboratively with the Court and the AB-PA Certified mental health professional in actively stabilizing the family's conflict and transition to a functional and healthy separated family structure.

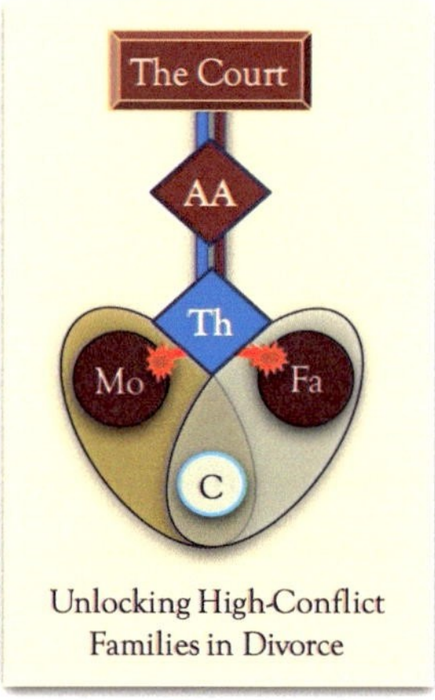

Formal training and Certification of select mental health professionals in AB-PA will provide the Court with the needed professional expertise to effectively assess, diagnose, treat, and resolve the attachment-related family pathology creating high-conflict divorce. Training of select attorneys within the family law system to serve as AB-PA Knowledgeable amicus attorneys for the Court will allow for the effective collaboration of the Court and the AB-PA Certified mental health professional in resolving the family conflict and stabilizing the family's transition to a functional and healthy separated family structure following divorce.

The Key to the solution is the teaming of an AB-PA Certified mental health professional with an AB-PA Knowledgeable amicus attorney who together can provide the Court with the necessary professional expertise needed to resolve the ongoing family conflict surrounding child custody issues that are the center of high-conflict divorce. This professional team of specialized mental health expertise and legal expertise regarding the nature and resolution of the family pathology of AB-PA can be consistently and regularly applied to each high-conflict family to stabilize the family's ongoing functioning and their transition to a stable and healthy separated family structure.

Treating and stabilizing the severity of the attachment-related family pathology creating AB-PA and the surrounding high-conflict divorce is not a short-term intervention. Instead, it requires ongoing treatment and active family stabilization from a mental health professional with specialized professional knowledge and expertise in the complex attachment-related pathology, personality disorder pathology, and family systems pathology creating the family conflict of AB-PA. Given the acknowledged treatment resistance of personality pathology, it is likely that these families will require years of active treatment stabilization, depending on the ages of the children and the need to ensure the children's healthy development free from being triangulated into ongoing family conflict.

The Key solution meets the needs of the children by ensuring that the children are allowed to have a normal-range and healthy childhood free from inter-parental conflict by effectively resolving inter-spousal conflict in the treatment-related setting of the AB-PA therapist's office rather than in the adversarial arena of the courtroom. Family problems and resolving inter-parental conflict is the domain of mental health treatment, not the legal system. The collaborative involvement of an AB-PA Knowledgeable amicus attorney with the professional expertise of an AB-PA Certified mental health professional can ensure the necessary mental health/legal system expertise and collaboration needed to support the treatment-related needs of the family.

Within this Key solution, each parent would still be able to retain separate legal representation if desired to ensure their legal rights, yet the focus of the Key solution is on helping the family develop the conflict-resolution skills needed to solve family conflict through collaborative negotiation and compromise rather than through litigation. The purpose of the Key solution is to provide the high-conflict family with the mental health support and expertise required to help the family make a successful transition to a healthy and functional separated family structure following divorce. The teaming of an AB-PA Certified mental health professional with an AB-PA Knowledgeable amicus attorney unlocks the high-conflict adversarial context of the legal system that will allow families to resolve their dysfunctional family relationship patterns with appropriate mental health expertise, support, and guidance, rather than through litigation.

Treatment-Focused Assessment

At the first indication of concern for possible attachment-related pathology within the family, the Court can order a **Treatment-Focused Assessment** from an AB-PA Certified mental health professional. Through the proposed pilot program, the training and Certification of select mental professionals in the attachment-related family pathology AB-PA will provide the Court with a pool of available AB-PA Certified mental health professionals (i.e., mental health professionals who possess the required professional expertise in attachment-related pathology, personality disorder pathology, family systems pathology, and complex trauma pathology) from whom the Court and the parties can select for conducting the structured Treatment-Focused Assessment protocol.

Following a six to eight-session structured clinical assessment protocol (Appendix 1: Treatment-Focused Assessment Protocol), the AB-PA Certified mental health professional produces a targeted data-driven treatment-focused report for the Court (Appendix 2: Sample Reports) regarding the treatment-related needs of the family, with specific recommendations for the steps required to resolve the family conflict.

Assembling the AB-PA Treatment Key

If the clinical data from the Treatment-Focused Assessment results in a recommendation from the mental health professional for assembling an AB-PA treatment Key, then the Court can assemble the treatment Key by teaming a new AB-PA Certified mental health professional (not the assessing mental health professional) with an AB-PA Knowledgeable amicus attorney.

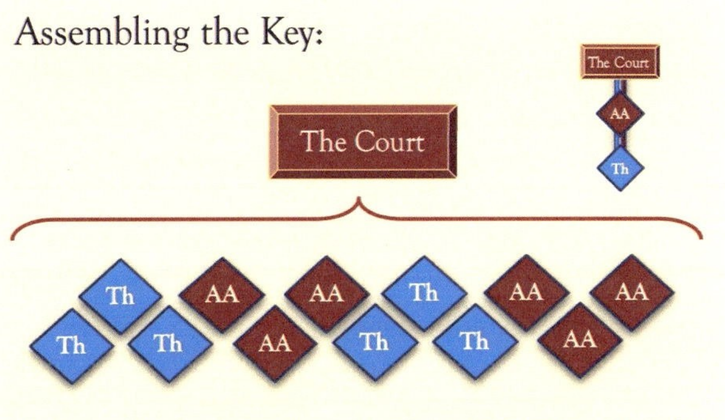

The Court will have an interchangeable pool of **AB-PA Knowledgeable** amicus attorneys and **AB-PA Certified** mental health professionals to draw from in assembling a key for each family.

The training and Certification program in the attachment-related family pathology of AB-PA will provide the Court with a pool of available AB-PA Certified mental health professionals and attorneys with the necessary professional expertise in attachment-related pathology, personality disorder pathology, family systems pathology, and complex trauma pathology needed to create the Key teaming of an AB-PA Certified mental health professional with an AB-PA Knowledgeable amicus attorney.

While the inherent adversarial structure of the legal system tends to support and feed existing conflict in families rather than reduce it, the teaming of an AB-PA Certified mental health professional with an AB-PA Knowledgeable amicus attorney creates a collaborative legal/mental health context that instead supports the resolution of family conflict rather than feeding it, while still allowing each party to retain separate legal counsel as desired to ensure protection of their legal rights. Training and Certification in AB-PA for mental health and legal professionals provides the Court with the professional expertise necessary to assemble a Key team of professional expertise from among the highest caliber of professionally trained and Certified mental health and legal professionals.

The Childress Institute Training & Certification in AB-PA

THE CHILDRESS INSTITUTE provides training and Certification in an attachment-based model of "parental alienation" (AB-PA) based on the seminal work of Dr. Craig Childress in this area (as described in his book, *An Attachment-Based Model of Parental Alienation: Foundations*).

The attachment-related pathology traditionally called "parental alienation" in the popular culture represents a complex psychological-family pathology involving the trans-generational transmission of attachment trauma from the childhood of the allied narcissistic/(borderline) personality parent to the current family relationships, mediated by the personality disorder pathology of the allied parent that is itself a product of this parent's childhood attachment trauma.

The attachment-related pathology evidenced in "parental alienation" represents a complex inter-play of four domains of pathology:

- Attachment-related pathology;
- Family systems pathology;
- Personality disorder pathology;
- Complex trauma.

Specialized training and professional expertise is required to appropriately assess, accurately diagnose, and effectively treat and resolve the family pathology of "parental-alienation" surrounding high-conflict divorce. In addition, this complex form of family pathology will typically require the involved stabilizing guidance of a knowledgeable and expert mental health professional for several years (depending on the ages of the children) in order to stabilize the pathology in the family and ensure a normal-range emotional and psychological environment for the children.

Mental health professionals who are assessing, diagnosing, and treating the attachment-related pathology creating high-conflict divorce need to be professionally knowledgeable and competent in the following domains:

- **The Attachment System:** Including internal working models (schemas) of attachment and the trans-generational transmission of attachment trauma, how the attachment system functions and how it characteristically dysfunctions, and the relationship of attachment trauma to the development of personality disorder pathology.

- **Personality Disorder Pathology:** How it develops, how it functions, and how it characteristically affects family relationships following divorce, including the role-reversal use of children as "regulatory objects" to stabilize the parent's personality pathology, and the manifestation of splitting pathology in family relationships.

- **Family Systems Therapy:** Including the family systems constructs of homeostasis and symptom development, triangulation of children into the spousal conflict, the formation and symptom indicators of a cross-generational coalition, and the development of emotional cutoffs in family relationships.

- **Complex Trauma:** The trans-generational transmission of attachment trauma through the creation of a false trauma reenactment narrative, and the differential diagnostic indicators of a false trauma reenactment narrative from an authentic response to current trauma.

THE CHILDRESS INSTITUTE provides a two-day **Basic Certification** program in AB-PA, and an additional 6-hour seminar for **Advanced Certification** in AB-PA for mental health professionals.

THE CHILDRESS INSTITUTE offers a one-day training program for legal professionals in the foundations of AB-PA that allows these legal professionals to effectively collaborate with the AB-PA Certified mental health professional in resolving the pathology.

Mental Health Professionals: Training and Certification in AB-PA

Basic Certification Content: A two-day Basic Certification seminar on the foundations, assessment, diagnosis, and treatment of the attachment-related family pathology of AB-PA.

Foundations of AB-PA: A professional-level description and analysis of the attachment-related origins of the pathology, the personality disorder origins of the pathology, and the family systems origins of the pathology.

Diagnosis of AB-PA: A professional-level description and analysis of the three diagnostic indicators of AB-PA and the 12 Associated Clinical Signs, as well as the diagnostic indicators of authentic versus inauthentic parent-child conflict and the symptom indicators of a cross-generational coalition that creates the child's symptoms.

Assessment of AB-PA: Professional-level instruction in conducting a six- to eight-session Treatment-Focused Assessment protocol, with descriptions of Key lines of clinical assessment inquiry during the three phases of the session Treatment-Focused Assessment protocol. Training in data-driven documentation and report writing for the Court, and data-driven diagnostic and treatment-related decision-making.

Treatment of AB-PA: Professional-level description of treatment-related approaches to restoring the child's normal-range attachment bonding motivations, including professional-level instruction in constructing and managing variations of a Strategic Family Systems Intervention (the *Contingent Visitation Schedule*) that can release the child from loyalty conflicts toward the parents without the need for a protective separation period. Training in data-driven decision-making in treatment is covered along with developing a Single-Case ABA design assessment and remedy intervention.

Advanced Certification Content: An additional one-day Advanced Seminar covers topics of professional expertise for Advanced Certification in AB-PA.

Attachment System Pathology: The one-day advanced seminar more fully examines the specific damaged information structures of the attachment system (including suppression of memory, identity, and executive function systems) and the trauma-created meme-structures of the pathogen that lead to the themes of AB-PA as expressed in the personality disorder pathology and family systems pathology of AB-PA.

Advanced Topics in Attachment Pathology: The advanced seminar illuminates additional aspects of the pathology, including malignant narcissism, gaslighting, the Dark Triad personality, infectious spread, and the associated attachment-related pathologies of cult formation and pathological hatred. Prior completion of Basic AB-PA Certification is required for Advanced Certification.

Legal Professionals: Foundations of AB-PA

AB-PA for Legal Professionals is a one-day seminar designed to provide educational training for legal professionals regarding the nature of the pathology and on collaborating with the AB-PA Certified mental health professional during both the initial phases of treatment and across the long-term stabilization of the high-conflict family.

The content of this one-day seminar covers mental health constructs but will not assume a prior mental health background. An additional focus of this one-day seminar is on the Court orders that may be needed at various phases of the family's recovery and long-term stabilization. This will include a description of the Strategic Family Systems Intervention (the *Contingent Visitation Schedule*) that may be enacted by the AB-PA Certified mental health professional, and the required Court orders to support this family systems intervention.

CPS Social Workers: AP-PA Specialists

The attachment-related family pathology of AB-PA can be identified by the presence of three specific diagnostic indicators in the child's symptom display:

1. **Attachment System Suppression:** The suppression of the child's attachment bonding motivations toward a normal-range and affectionally available parent.
2. **Personality Disorder Traits or Phobic Anxiety:** The presence in the child's symptom display of five a-priori predicted narcissistic and borderline personality disorder traits, or a phobic anxiety toward a normal-range and affectionally available parent.
3. **Encapsulated Persecutory Delusion:** The child displays a fixed and false belief that is maintained despite contrary evidence (a delusion) regarding the child's supposed "victimization" by the normal-range parenting of the targeted parent.

Pathogenic parenting[16] by the allied parent that is creating significant developmental pathology in the child (diagnostic indicator 1), personality pathology or a phobic anxiety disorder in the child (diagnostic indicator 2), and delusional-psychiatric pathology in the child (diagnostic indicator 3) represents a DSM-5 diagnosis of V995.51 Child Psychological Abuse, Confirmed.

A confirmed DSM-5 diagnosis of V995.51 Child Psychological Abuse activates the mental health professional's "duty to protect" and mandated child abuse reporting obligations. Child Protective Service social workers who receive and investigate suspected child abuse reports from mental health professionals that include a confirmed DSM-5 diagnosis of V995.51 Child Psychological Abuse will need to know how to properly assess and identify the attachment-related pathology of AB-PA.

The AB-PA Specialist training for CPS social workers is designed to provide a broad understanding for all CPS social workers regarding the foundations of the pathology, and more specific

[16] Patho=pathology; genic=genesis. Pathogenic parenting is a defined construct in both developmental and clinical psychology to describe the creation of significant psychopathology in the child through aberrant and distorted parenting practices.

intensive training for a select set of CPS social workers (AB-PA Specialists within the CPS system) regarding assessment and diagnosis of AB-PA and collaboration with the AB-PA Certified mental health professional and AB-PA knowledgeable amicus attorney in resolving the family pathology.

A Comprehensive Mental Health Solution

The professional expertise made available to the Court from the Key solution of teaming an AB-PA Certified mental health professional with an AB-PA Knowledgeable amicus attorney represents a comprehensive and long-term solution to the family pathology creating high-conflict divorce. A pilot program in the family courts that incorporates evidence-based outcome data will provide a demonstration of the effectiveness of a comprehensive and integrated approach to resolving high-conflict divorce through the collaboration of mental health expertise with the family courts, eliminating the need for the continued and excessive litigation currently surrounding high-conflict families.

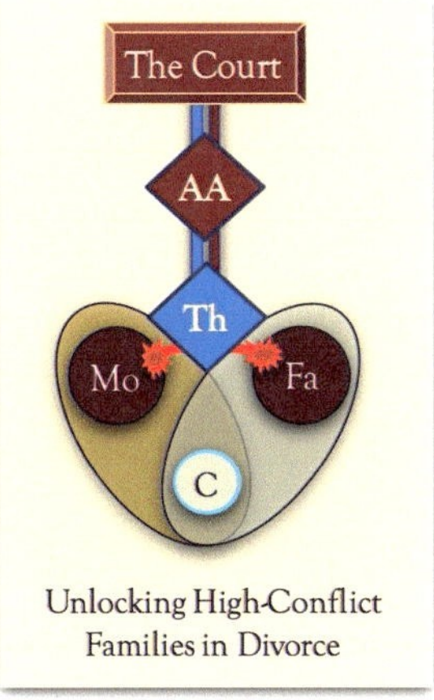

This Key solution is made available by a return to established constructs and principles of professional psychology in the assessment, diagnosis, and treatment of family pathology. The attachment-related family pathology of AB-PA is complex and challenging, but it is solvable once we return to the established standards of practice for professional psychology. The Treatment-Focused Assessment protocol and the Key solution provide for data-driven decision making in resolving family pathology and protecting children from becoming caught in the inter-spousal conflict of their parents.

Children have the right of childhood to love both parents, and to receive the love of both parents in return. The Key solution to AB-PA and high-conflict families protects children from becoming caught in their parent's spousal conflicts, and it allows children to return to their normal-range childhood, freed from the inter-spousal conflicts of their parents surrounding the divorce.

Program Evaluation Data

The collection of program evaluation data is integrated into the Key solution (Appendices 3-7). The family intervention begins with an initial Treatment-Focused Assessment (Appendix 1) that documents the child's symptoms using the *Diagnostic Checklist for Pathogenic Parenting* (Appendix 4) and the *Parenting Practices Rating Scale* (Appendix 5). During the family's participation in the AB-PA Key solution, daily/weekly parent and therapist-generated collaborative family ratings of the child's symptoms using the *Parent-Child Relationship Rating Scale* (Appendix 6) document the child's symptoms and allow for data-driven decision-making and monitoring of progress toward treatment goals. Additional Outcome Data (Appendix 7) is collected at six-month intervals during the family's participation in the AB-PA Key solution that documents the perceptions of the parents, of the AB-PA Certified therapist, and of the AB-PA Knowledgeable amicus attorney regarding the family's participation in the AB-PA Key program and progress toward treatment goals.

Appendix 1: Treatment-Focused Assessment Protocol

Treatment-Focused Assessment Protocol

Diagnostic Indicators of AB-PA

Every form of child pathology will evidence a specific and distinctive pattern of symptoms. The trans-generational transmission of *pathological mourning* (Bowlby) from the allied narcissistic (or borderline) personality parent (Beck, Kernberg, Millon) in a cross-generational coalition with the child against the other parent (Haley; Minuchin) is no exception. The pathogenic parenting of an allied parent that creates the child's rejection of a normal-range and affectionally available parent following divorce will be reflected in a set of three definitive diagnostic indicators in the child's symptom display (Childress, 2015):

1.) Attachment System Suppression. The child will evidence a suppression of normal-range attachment bonding motivations toward a normal-range and affectionally available parent. This child symptom identifies the family pathology as an attachment-related form of pathology.

2.) Personality Disorder Symptoms: The child's symptom display will evidence a set of five a-priori predicted narcissistic personality traits directed toward the targeted parent. These narcissistic personality features in the child's symptom display represent the "psychological fingerprint" evidence of the psychological control of the child by a narcissistic/(borderline) parent. The *primary case* for these narcissistic personality traits is the allied parent who is transferring these deviant attitudes and beliefs to the child through this parent's psychological influence and psychological control of the child. In some cases, the child might evidence an extreme anxiety in response to the targeted-rejected parent that will meet DSM-5 diagnostic criteria for a Specific Phobia, but of a bizarre and unrealistic "father type" or "mother type."

3.) Encapsulated Persecutory Delusion. The child symptoms will evidence a fixed-and-false belief that is maintained despite contrary evidence (i.e., a delusion) regarding the child's supposed "victimization" by the normal-range parenting of the targeted parent. This symptom evidenced by the child represents an encapsulated persecutory delusion. As with the narcissistic symptoms, the *primary case* for this encapsulated persecutory delusion is the allied narcissistic/(borderline) personality parent, and the origins of this fixed and false belief is in the "internal working models" (schemas) of this parent's childhood attachment trauma

A treatment-focused clinical assessment of the pathogenic parenting associated with the trans-generational transmission of disordered mourning should assess for and document the presence or absence of these three diagnostic features in the child's symptom display. The ***Diagnostic Checklist for Pathogenic Parenting*** (Appendix 2) represents a structured method for documenting the presence or absence of these three diagnostic symptom indicators in the child's symptom display.

Parenting Practices Assessment

In addition to documenting the child's symptom features, the normal-range or problematic parenting of the targeted-rejected parent should also be assessed and documented. The **Parenting Practices Rating Scale** (Appendix 3) is designed to document the results of the clinical assessment regarding the parenting practices of the targeted-rejected parent. Normal-range parenting on the Parenting Practices Rating Scale would be parenting at Levels 3 and 4 along with a rating on the *Permissive to Authoritarian Dimension* within the range from 25 to 75. These ratings of parenting practices are based on the clinical judgement of the assessing mental health professional and are a means to document this professional clinical judgement.

Treatment-Focused Assessment Protocol: Session Structure

The clinical assessment process is conducted across a set of six to eight targeted clinical assessment sessions.

- **Initial Sessions:** The initial two treatment-focused clinical assessment sessions are to collect history and symptom information from each parent individually.

- **Direct Assessment:** The middle two sessions are a direct assessment of the child's symptoms, either in individual clinical interviews with the child or in parent-child dyadic sessions with the child and targeted parent (at least one dyadic session should be conducted). Clinical probes of the child's symptom features during these sessions can help illuminate the child's symptom display.

- **Parent Response:** The final two sessions are feedback sessions provided to each of the parents to assess the "schemas" of each parent in response to the clinical findings from the prior sessions.

Additional sessions can be added if needed, but typically six to eight sessions should be sufficient to document the presence or absence of the diagnostic indicators of pathogenic parenting associated with the attachment-related pathology of disordered mourning.

Treatment-Focused Report Format

Treatment-focused assessments will produce a targeted report for the Court regarding the treatment requirements needed to resolve the family pathology. Two examples of the type of report available from a treatment-focused assessment protocol, one for a confirmed diagnosis of pathogenic parenting and one for a sub-threshold display of child symptoms, are contained in Appendix 4.

In reports to the Court, it is recommended that the *Diagnostic Checklist for Pathogenic Parenting* and the *Parenting Practices Rating Scale* be included with the report for review by the Court in its decision-making function.

Summary of Treatment-Focused Assessment Structure

The treatment-focused clinical assessment uses the following protocol:

1.) **Focus of Assessment:** To assess for the attachment-related pathology of disordered mourning (Bowlby) involving an allied narcissistic/(borderline) parent (Beck; Kernberg; Millon) who is in a cross-generational coalition with the child against the other parent (Minuchin; Haley).

2.) **Diagnostic Checklist for Pathogenic Parenting:** To document the child's symptom features of clinical concern relative to the potential of *pathogenic parenting*.

3.) **Parenting Practices Rating Scale:** To document the normal-range parenting of the targeted-rejected parent or document areas of problematic parenting concern to be addressed in the treatment plan.

4.) **Assessment Session Structure:** A set of six to eight clinical assessment sessions are recommended to document the presence or absence of the diagnostic indicators of pathogenic parenting by an allied narcissistic/(borderline) parent.

Appendix 2: Sample Treatment-Focused Assessment Reports

A Treatment-Focused Assessment Report Example for a Confirmed Diagnosis of Pathogenic Parenting

Date: <Date of Assessment>
Psychologist: <Psychologist's Name>

Scope of Report

A Treatment-Focused Assessment was requested by the Court for the parent-child relationship of John Doe (DOB: 1/15/08) with his mother regarding their estranged and conflictual relationship. This treatment-focused assessment report is based on the following family interviews:

<date>: Clinical interview with mother
<date>: Clinical interview with father
<date>: Clinical interview with child
<date>: Clinical relationship assessment with mother and child
<date>: Clinical interview with mother
<date>: Clinical relationship assessment with mother and child
<date>: Clinical interview with father

Rating Scales Completed (attached)

Parenting Practices Rating Scale (mother)
Diagnostic Checklist for Pathogenic Parenting

Results of Assessment

Based on the clinical assessments, the child displays the three symptom indicators of pathogenic parenting associated with an attachment-based model of "parental alienation" (AB-PA; Childress, 2015):

1) **Attachment System Suppression:** A targeted and selective suppression of the child's attachment bonding motivations relative to his mother in the absence of sufficiently distorted parenting practices from the mother that would account for the suppression of the child's attachment system;

2) **Personality Disorder Traits:** A set of five specific narcissistic/borderline personality disorder features are present in the child's symptom display;

3) **Encapsulated Delusional Belief System:** The child evidences an intransigently held fixed and false belief that is maintained despite contrary evidence (i.e., an encapsulated delusion) regarding the child's supposed "victimization" by the normal-range parenting of the mother(i.e., an encapsulated persecutory delusion).

The presence of this specific symptom pattern in a child's symptom display is consistent with an attachment-based framework for conceptualizing "parental alienation" processes within the family that involve an induced suppression of the child's attachment bonding motivations toward a normal-range and affectionally available parent (i.e., the targeted parent) as a result of the distorted parenting practices of a personality disordered parent (i.e., narcissistic/borderline features, which accounts for the presence of these features in the child's symptom display).

The mother's parenting practices on the Parenting Practices Rating Scale are assessed to be broadly normal-range. The mother's parenting would be classified as Level 4, Positive Parenting; Affectionate Involvement – Structured Spectrum. The mother establishes clearly defined rules and expectations for child behavior that are well within normal-range parenting, and the mother's delivery of consequences is fair and is based on these established rules and expectations for child behavior. The mother offers parental encouragement and affection, but these offers of parental affection are typically rejected by the child. The mother's rating on the Permissive to Authoritarian Dimension would be 60, which is well within normal-range parenting. She tends toward the use of clearly established rules and appropriate parental discipline for child non-compliance. The mother's capacity for authentic empathy is normal-range. She is able to self-reflect on her actions and also de-center from her own perspective to adopt the frame of reference of other people. She is not overly self-involved nor does she project her own emotional needs into and onto the child. There are no issues of clinical concern regarding the mother's parenting.

DSM-5 Diagnosis

The combined presence in the child's symptom display of significant attachment-related developmental pathology (diagnostic indicator 1), narcissistic personality disorder pathology (diagnostic indicator 2), and delusional-psychiatric pathology (diagnostic indicator 3) represents definitive diagnostic evidence of pathogenic parenting by an allied parent with prominent narcissistic and/or borderline personality traits, since no other pathology will account for this specific symptom pattern other than pathogenic parenting by an allied narcissistic/borderline personality parent. This set of severe child symptoms warrants the following DSM-5 diagnosis for the child:

309.4 Adjustment Disorder with mixed disturbance of emotions and conduct

V61.20 Parent-Child Relational Problem

V61.29 Child Affected by Parental Relationship Distress

V995.51 Child Psychological Abuse, Confirmed (pathogenic parenting)

Treatment Indications

A confirmed DSM-5 diagnosis of Child Psychological Abuse warrants the following child protection and treatment response:

1.) Protective Separation Period: A period of protective separation of the child from the psychologically abusive parenting practices of the allied parent is required in order to protect the child from ongoing exposure to psychologically abusive parenting practices and allow for the treatment and recovery of the child's normal-range and healthy development. Attempting therapy without first establishing a period of protective separation from the pathogenic parenting practices of the father will continue the child's ongoing exposure to the psychologically abusive parenting of the father that is creating significant developmental pathology, personality disorder pathology, and delusional-psychiatric pathology in the child, and will lead to the child becoming a "psychological battleground" between the treatment goals of restoring the child's healthy and normal-range development and the continuing pathogenic goals of the father to create and maintain the child's pathology.

2.) Treatment: Appropriate parent-child psychotherapy should be initiated to recover and heal the damaged parent-child affectional bond with the mother and resolve the impact of the prior psychological abuse inflicted on the child by the father's distorted and psychologically abusive parenting practices in order to restore the child's healthy emotional and psychological development.

3.) Collateral Therapy: The father should be required to obtain collateral individual therapy with the treatment goal of fostering insight into the cause of the prior abusive parenting practices.

4.) End of Protective Separation: The protective separation period should be ended once the child's symptoms associated with the prior psychologically abusive parenting practices of the father are successfully resolved and the child's recovery is stabilized.

5.) Restoration of the Relationship with the Abusive Parent: The restoration of the child's relationship with the formerly abusive parent should include sufficient safeguards to ensure that the psychological abuse of the child does not resume once contact with the father is restored. The demonstrated cooperation of the father with his individual collateral therapy and his demonstrated insight into the cause of the prior psychological abuse of the child would represent important considerations in the level of safeguards needed to ensure the child's protection.

6.) Relapse: If the child's symptoms reoccur once the child's contact with the father is restored, then another period of protective separation will be needed in order to again recover the child's normal-range and healthy development, and additional protective safeguards will be warranted prior to once again exposing the child to the pathogenic parenting practices of the father.

Child Response to a Protective Separation

The child may initially respond to a protective separation from the currently allied parent (i.e., the father) with increased protest behavior and defiance. This child response represents an emotional-behavioral tantrum reflecting the child's currently over-empowered status relative to accepting authority (i.e. both parental authority and the authority of the Court). Responding to emotional displays of child tantrum behaviors with calm and steady purpose that restores the child to an appropriate social and family hierarchy of cooperation with Court and parental authority will be important to supporting successful family therapy and the resolution of the child's symptoms. Any concern regarding the child's expressed distress at the protective separation from the currently allied parent (i.e., the father) should recognize that the child is fully capable of ending the protective separation period by becoming non-symptomatic. If the child wishes a termination of the protective separation period, then the child simply needs to evidence normal-range affectional child behavior in response to the normal-range parenting practices of the mother, which is under the treatment-related monitoring of the family therapist.

Ending the Protective Separation Period

The protective separation period from the pathogenic and psychologically abusive parenting practices of the allied parent should be ended upon the successful treatment and resolution of the child's symptoms and restoration of the child's healthy and normal-range development. The treating family therapist should seek Court approval to end the child's protective separation from the pathogenic parenting practices of the currently allied parent (i.e., the father) based on the treatment-related gains achieved. Progress reports to the parents and to the Court from the treating family therapist should be provided at least every six months.

Sincerely,

<psychologist signature>
Psychologist, <license number>

A Treatment-Focused Assessment Report Example for
Sub-Threshold Symptoms for the Diagnosis of Pathogenic Parenting

Date: <Date>
Psychologist: <Psychologist's Name>

Scope of Report

A treatment-focused assessment was requested by the Court for the parent-child relationship of John Doe (DOB: 1/15/08) with his mother regarding their estranged and conflictual relationship. This treatment-focused assessment report is based on the following family interviews:

<date>: Clinical interview with mother
<date>: Clinical interview with father
<date>: Clinical interview with child
<date>: Clinical relationship assessment with mother and child
<date>: Clinical interview with mother
<date>: Clinical relationship assessment with mother and child
<date>: Clinical interview with father

Rating Scales Completed (attached)

Parenting Practices Rating Scale (mother)
Diagnostic Checklist for Pathogenic Parenting

Results of Assessment

Based on the clinical assessments, the child does not display the three symptom indicators of pathogenic parenting associated with an attachment-based model of "parental alienation" (AB-PA; Childress, 2015):

1) **Attachment System Suppression:** A targeted and selective suppression of the child's attachment bonding motivations relative to his mother in the absence of sufficiently distorted parenting practices from the mother that would account for the suppression of the child's attachment system;

2) **Personality Disorder Traits:** A set of five specific narcissistic/borderline personality disorder features are present in the child's symptom display;

3) **Encapsulated Delusional Belief System:** The child evidences an intransigently held fixed and false belief that is maintained despite contrary evidence (i.e., an encapsulated delusion) regarding the child's supposed "victimization" by the normal-range parenting of the mother(i.e., an encapsulated persecutory delusion).

The child's symptom presentation does not fully evidence an intransigently held fixed-and-false belief in the child's supposed "victimization" because the mother's parenting practices are sufficiently problematic to warrant concerns that the child's perceptions of his mother have some component of accuracy. In addition, John expressed an openness to restoring a relationship with his mother if his potentially reality-based concerns can be adequately addressed.

However, John also evidenced a prominent suppression of normal-range attachment bonding motivation toward his mother and he displayed prominent signs of narcissistic personality disorder features in his attitude and responses to his mother. The symptom features in the family also evidenced several Associated Clinical Signs (see attached Diagnostic Checklist for Pathogenic Parenting), so that concerns regarding the potential pathogenic influence of the currently allied and supposedly "favored" parent (i.e., the father) continue.

Mother's Parenting Practices

The mother's parenting practices are assessed to be in the Level 3 domain on the Parenting Practices Rating Scale (Problematic Parenting), reflecting potentially harsh discipline (Item 12) and high-anger parenting (Item 13). These parenting practices, however, may also be a product of the child's provoking these parenting responses through a high level of child non-compliance and disrespect for parental authority. A Response-to-Intervention assessment would help clarify the causal direction for the parent-child conflict.

The child is also likely impacted by chronic exposure to high levels of inter-spousal conflict involving intermittent explosive anger from one spouse directed toward the other spouse (Item 16). While this inter-spousal anger is not directed toward the child, the extent of the high inter-spousal conflict likely creates considerable stress for the child and represents a degree of parental insensitivity for the child's emotional and psychological needs by at least one, and possibly both, parents. Restricting the expression of inter-spousal anger and developing cooperative co-parenting spousal skills of respecting boundaries and for mutual displays of kindness in respectful communication would be in the emotional and psychological best interests of the child.

The mother appears to employ a more disciplinarian approach to parenting involving structured rules and consequences, and her rating on the Permissive to Authoritarian Dimension would be in the 60 to 70 range, which is in the normal-range of parenting. A reduction in parent-child conflict might be achieved by helping the mother expand her parenting options by using increased dialogue and negotiation skills that would shift her rating on the Permissive to Authoritarian Dimension into the mid-range of 45 to 55. However, it should also be noted that the mother's current parenting practices are well within the normal-range for parenting generally, and considerable latitude should be granted to parents to establish rules and values within their families that are consistent with their cultural and personal value systems.

The mother's capacity for authentic empathy with the child appears to be in the normal range. She is able to self-reflect on her own behavior and she is also able to de-center from her own perspective to view situations from alternate points of view. The mother does not appear to become overly self-involved in needing to have her perspective validated, nor does she appear to project her own needs onto the child.

There are no areas of clinical concern related to the mother's parenting.

Treatment Indications

Based on the set of symptom features in child's symptom display and the assessment of the mother's current parenting practices, a Response-to-Intervention (RTI) treatment approach is recommended for a 6-month period to further assess the role of the mother's parenting practices relative to the potential role of pathogenic parental influence from the father in creating and supporting the child's symptomatic relationship with his mother.

1.) Response to Intervention (RTI) Assessment

A 6-month period of family therapy is recommended that includes both mother-child therapy sessions to improve communication and conflict resolution skills as well as collateral sessions with the mother to expand and improve her parenting responses to John.

Authentic Parent-Child Conflict-Resolution: If the mother displays normal-range and appropriate parenting in response to treatment directives, then John's behavior toward his mother should show corresponding improvement (i.e., demonstrating that the child's behavior is under the "stimulus control" of the parent's behavior, meaning that the parent-child conflict is authentic to their relationship features). Changes to the mother's parenting practices will then lead to a resolution of the parent-child conflict.

Authentic Parent-Child Conflict–No Resolution: If the mother is unable to sufficiently alter her potentially harsh discipline and high-anger parenting behavior in response to treatment directives, then this would represent suggestive clinical evidence that the source of the mother-son conflict is potentially authentic to their relationship dynamics, and family therapy should continue to seek changes in the mother's parenting responses toward a more nurturing and affectionate parenting approach to help resolve the parent-child conflict.

Inauthentic Parent-Child Conflict: If, however, the mother displays normal-range and appropriate parenting in response to treatment directives, and John's symptoms continue despite changes in the mother's parenting practices, then this would represent confirming diagnostic evidence that John's behavior is not under the "stimulus control" of his mother's behavior and her responses to him, meaning that he is not responding to authentic difficulties in the mother-son relationship. The continuance of John's symptomatic behavior toward his mother despite changes in the mother's parenting practices would represent diagnostic evidence that John's symptomatic responses to his mother are likely being created by the pathogenic parenting practices of the father (through the formation of a cross-generational coalition of the child with his father against the mother). A Response-to-Intervention treatment plan to address the pathogenic parenting of the father in creating the child's ongoing conflict with the mother should then be developed and implemented.

2.) Compliance with Court Orders for Custody and Visitation

All parties, including the child, should comply fully with all Court orders including those for custody and visitation. Failure by the currently allied and supposedly "favored" parent (i.e., the father) to comply with Court orders for custody and visitation should be viewed as non-compliance with treatment, and a follow-up treatment-focused assessment should be initiated (at the written recommendation of the treating family therapist) to determine whether a protective separation of the child from the potentially pathogenic parenting practices of the father is needed to allow for effective treatment.

Child noncompliance with Court orders for custody and visitation, such as refusing custody time-share visitations with the mother, should be ascribed as a serious failure in parenting by the currently allied and supposedly "favored" parent (i.e., the father) representing a parental failure to demonstrate appropriate parental responsibility.

- If the father is instructing the child to comply with the father's directive to cooperate with the mother's custody and visitation time and the child is refusing to comply with the father's directive, then the child is evidencing oppositional non-compliant behavior relative to the father's parental authority and the authority of the Court.

- As the allied and supposedly "favored" parent, the child's behavior is a reflection of the parenting received from the father, so that the child's oppositional non-compliance with the father's parental authority and the authority of the Court is a direct reflection on the father's parenting and his capacity for providing appropriate parental guidance to the child.

A failure to exercise effective parental responsibility and guidance by the allied and supposedly "favored" parent should be viewed as representing the father's non-compliance with the requirements of treatment by failing to exercise appropriate parental responsibility and child guidance as the "favored" and allied parent. The child's refusal to comply with Court orders, including all orders for custody and visitation, and the child's direct defiance of the father's parental authority should trigger a follow-up treatment-focused assessment (at the written recommendation of the treating family therapist) to determine whether a change in the responsible parent is needed to allow for effective treatment and the recovery of the child's normal-range and healthy development.

In any follow-up treatment-focused assessment, primary consideration should be afforded to the treatment needs of the child in establishing the treatment-related conditions necessary for effective treatment. The treatment-related needs of the child should be given precedence over parental considerations of being "favored" or "unfavored" by the child. If the allied and supposedly "favored" parent cannot establish the conditions necessary for the effective resolution of the child's symptoms, then a change in the responsible parent may be necessary due to the then demonstrated parental failure of the allied and supposedly "favored" parent to enact the appropriate parental authority and guidance necessary for the child's successful treatment.

Progress reports to the parents and to the Court from the treating family therapist should be provided at least every six months.

Sincerely,

<psychologist signature>
Psychologist, <license number>

Appendix 3: Program Evaluation

AB-PA Key Intervention
Program Evaluation

1. Initial Family Data

Each family's participation in the AB-PA Key Intervention program begins with a treatment-related assessment that will produce a written treatment plan specifying measureable treatment goals for achieving normal-range parent-child relationships, as measured by the *Parent-Child Relationship Rating Scale* (Appendix 6).

The initial Treatment-Focused Assessment will document:

Child Symptoms: Using the *Diagnostic Checklist for Pathogenic Parenting* (Appendix 4)

Parenting Behaviors: Using the *Parenting Practices Rating Scale* (Appendix 5)

2. Treatment Data:

During treatment, collaborative weekly data is collected regarding child symptoms.

Child's Symptoms: Weekly parent-generated and therapist-generated collaborative family ratings using the *Parent-Child Relationship Rating Scale* will monitor progress toward treatment goals and be used in possible triggering of the treatment-related Contingent Visitation Schedule as needed.

Parenting Behaviors: If a change in parenting behaviors is indicated as part of the written treatment plan, then periodic (3-month) assessments of parenting practices using the *Parenting Practices Rating Scale* will monitor progress toward this goal.

Treatment-Related Data: If a treatment-related Contingent Visitation Schedule is employed with the family, then the triggering, enactment, and termination of treatment-related Contingent Visitation Schedule will be in response to the child's symptoms as documented on weekly therapist-generated collaborative family ratings using the *Parent-Child Relationship Rating Scale*.

3. Scheduled Outcome Feedback Data

At six-month intervals throughout the family's involvement in the AB-PA Key Solution program, each parent, the AB-PA therapist, and the AB-PA amicus attorney will complete outcome feedback questionnaires (Appendix 7).

Appendix 4: Diagnostic Checklist for Pathogenic Parenting

Diagnostic Checklist for Pathogenic Parenting: Extended Version

C.A. Childress, Psy.D. (2015/2017)

All three of the diagnostic indicators must be present (either 2a OR 2b) for a clinical diagnosis of attachment-based "parental alienation." Sub-threshold clinical presentations can be further evaluated using a "Response to Intervention" trial.

1. Attachment System Suppression

Present	Sub-Threshold	Absent	
☐	☐	☐	The child's symptoms evidence a selective and targeted suppression of the normal-range functioning of the child's attachment bonding motivations toward one parent, the targeted-rejected parent, in which the child seeks to entirely terminate a relationship with this parent (i.e., a child-initiated cutoff in the child's relationship with a normal-range and affectionally available parent).

Secondary Criterion: **Normal-Range Parenting:**

yes	no	
☐	☐	The parenting practices of the targeted-rejected parent are assessed to be broadly normal-range, with due consideration given to the wide spectrum of acceptable parenting that is typically displayed in normal-range families.

Normal-range parenting includes the legitimate exercise of parental prerogatives in establishing desired family values through parental expectations for desired child behavior and normal-range discipline practices.

2(a). Personality Disorder Traits

Present	Sub-Threshold	Absent	
☐	☐	☐	The child's symptoms evidence all five of the following narcissistic/(borderline) personality disorder features displayed toward the targeted-rejected parent.

Sub-Criterion Met

yes	no	
☐	☐	**Grandiosity:** The child displays a grandiose perception of occupying an inappropriately elevated status in the family hierarchy that is above the targeted-rejected parent from which the child feels empowered to sit in judgment of the targeted-rejected parent as both a parent and as a person.
☐	☐	**Absence of Empathy:** The child displays a complete absence of empathy for the emotional pain being inflicted on the targeted-rejected parent by the child's hostility and rejection of this parent.
☐	☐	**Entitlement:** The child displays an over-empowered sense of entitlement in which the child expects that his or her desires will be met by the targeted-rejected parent to the child's satisfaction, and if the rejected parent fails to meet the child's entitled expectations to the child's satisfaction then the child feels entitled to enact a retaliatory punishment on the rejected parent for the child's judgment of parental failures
☐	☐	**Haughty and Arrogant Attitude:** The child displays an attitude of haughty arrogance and contemptuous disdain for the targeted-rejected parent.
☐	☐	**Splitting:** The child evidences polarized extremes of attitude toward the parents, in which the supposedly "favored" parent is idealized as the all-good and nurturing parent while the rejected parent is entirely devalued as the all-bad and entirely inadequate parent.

2(b). Phobic Anxiety Toward a Parent

Present	Sub-Threshold	Absent	
☐	☐	☐	The child's symptoms evidence an extreme and excessive anxiety toward the targeted-rejected parent that meets the following DSM-5 diagnostic criteria for a specific phobia:

Criterion Met

yes	no	
☐	☐	**Persistent Unwarranted Fear**: The child displays a persistent and unwarranted fear of the targeted-rejected parent that is cued either by the presence of the targeted parent or in anticipation of being in the presence of the targeted parent
☐	☐	**Severe Anxiety Response:** The presence of the targeted-rejected parent almost invariably provokes an anxiety response which can reach the levels of a situationally provoked panic attack.
☐	☐	**Avoidance of Parent:** The child seeks to avoid exposure to the targeted parent due to the situationally provoked anxiety or else endures the presence of the targeted parent with great distress.

3. Fixed False Belief

Present	Sub-Threshold	Absent	
☐	☐	☐	The child's symptoms display an intransigently held, fixed and false belief maintained despite contrary evidence (a delusion) regarding the child's supposed "victimization" by the normal-range parenting of the targeted-rejected parent (an encapsulated persecutory delusion). The child's beliefs carry the implication that the normal-range parenting of the targeted-rejected parent are somehow "abusive" toward the child. The parenting practices of the targeted-rejected parent are assessed to be broadly normal-range.

DSM-5 Diagnosis

If the three diagnostic indicators of attachment-based "parental alienation" are present in the child's symptom display (either 2a or 2b), the appropriate DSM-5 diagnosis is:

DSM-5 Diagnosis

309.4 Adjustment Disorder with mixed disturbance of emotions and conduct

V61.20 Parent-Child Relational Problem

V61.29 Child Affected by Parental Relationship Distress

V995.51 Child Psychological Abuse, Confirmed (pathogenic parenting)

Checklist of Associated Clinical Signs (ACS)

evident	not evident	
☐	☐	ACS 1: Use of the Word "Forced"
☐	☐	ACS 2: Enhancing Child Empowerment to Reject the Other Parent

evident	not evident	
☐	☐	"Child should decide on visitation"
☐	☐	"Listen to the child"
☐	☐	Advocating for child testimony

☐	☐	ACS 3: The Exclusion Demand
☐	☐	ACS 4: Parental Replacement
☐	☐	ACS 5: The Unforgivable Event
☐	☐	ACS 6: Liar – Fake
☐	☐	ACS 7: Themes for Rejection

evident	not evident	
☐	☐	Too Controlling
☐	☐	Anger management
☐	☐	Targeted parent doesn't take responsibility/apologize
☐	☐	New romantic relationship neglects the child
☐	☐	Prior neglect of the child by the parent
☐	☐	Vague personhood of the targeted parent
☐	☐	Non-forgivable grudge
☐	☐	Not feeding the child

☐	☐	ACS 8: Unwarranted Use of the Word "Abuse"
☐	☐	ACS 9: Excessive Texting, Phone Calls, and Emails
☐	☐	ACS 10: Role-Reversal Use of the Child ("It's not me, it's the child who...")
☐	☐	ACS 11: Targeted Parent "Deserves to be Rejected"
☐	☐	ACS 12: Allied Parent Disregards Court Orders and Court Authority

evident	not evident	
☐	☐	Child disregard of court orders for custody
☐	☐	Child runaway behavior from the targeted parent

Appendix 5: Parenting Practices Rating Scale

Parenting Practices Rating Scale

C.A Childress, Psy.D. (2016)

Name of Parent: ______________________ Date: ____________

Name of Rater: ______________________

Indicate all that apply.

Child Abuse Ratings: Do not indicate child abuse is present unless allegations have been confirmed. In cases of abuse allegations that have neither been confirmed nor disconfirmed, or that are unfounded, use Allegation subheading rating not Category rating.

Level 1: Child Abuse

☐ 1. **Sexual Abuse**

As defined by legal statute.

- ☐ Allegation: Neither confirmed nor disconfirmed
- ☐ Allegation: Unfounded

☐ 2. **Physical Abuse**

Hitting the child with a closed fist; striking the child with an open hand or a closed fist around the head or shoulders; striking the child with sufficient force to leave bruises; striking the child with any instrument (weapon) such as kitchen utensils, paddles, straps, belts, or cords.

- ☐ Allegation: Neither confirmed nor disconfirmed
- ☐ Allegation: Unfounded

☐ 3. **Emotional Abuse**

Frequent verbal degradation of the child as a person in a hostile and demeaning tone; frequent humiliation of the child.

- ☐ Allegation: Neither confirmed nor disconfirmed
- ☐ Allegation: Unfounded

☐ 4. **Psychological Abuse**

Pathogenic parenting that creates significant psychological or developmental pathology in the child in order to meet the emotional and psychological needs of the parent, including a role-reversal use of the child as a regulatory object for the parent's emotional and psychological needs.

- ☐ Allegation: Neither confirmed nor disconfirmed
- ☐ Allegation: Unfounded

☐ 5. **Neglect**

Failure to provide for the child's basic needs for food, shelter, safety, and general care.

- ☐ Allegation: Neither confirmed nor disconfirmed
- ☐ Allegation: Unfounded

☐ 6. **Domestic Violence Exposure**

Repeated traumatic exposure of the child to one parent's violent physical assaults toward the other parent or to the repeated emotional degradation (emotional abuse) of the other parent.

- ☐ Allegation: Neither confirmed nor disconfirmed
- ☐ Allegation: Unfounded

Level 2: Severely Problematic Parenting

☐ 7. **Overly Strict Discipline**
Parental discipline practices that are excessively harsh and over-controlling, such as inflicting severe physical discomfort on the child through the use of stress postures, using shaming techniques, or confining the child in an enclosed area for excessively long periods (room time-outs are not overly strict discipline).

☐ 8. **Overly Hostile Parenting**
Frequent displays (more days than not) of excessive parental anger (a 6 or above on a 10-point subjective scale).

☐ 9. **Overly Disengaged Parenting**
Repeated failure to provide parental supervision and/or age-appropriate limits on the child's behavior and activities; parental major depression or substance abuse problems.

☐ 10.. **Overly Involved-Intrusive Parenting**
Enmeshed, over-intrusive, and/or over-anxious parenting that violates the psychological self-integrity of the child; role-reversal use of the child as a regulatory object for the parent's anxiety or narcissistic needs.

☐ 11. **Family Context of High Inter-Spousal Conflict**
Repeated exposure of the child to high inter-spousal conflict that includes excessive displays of inter-spousal anger.

Level 3: Problematic Parenting

☐ 12. **Harsh Discipline**
Excessive use of strict discipline practices in the context of limited displays of parental affection; limited use of parental praise, encouragement, and expressions of appreciation.

☐ 13. **High-Anger Parenting**
Chronic parental irritability and anger and minimal expressions of parental affection.

☐ 14. **Uninvolved Parenting**
Disinterested lack of involvement with the child; emotionally disengaged parenting; parental depression.

☐ 15. **Anxious or Over-Involved Parenting**
Intrusive parenting that does not respect interpersonal boundaries.

☐ 16. **Overwhelmed Parenting**
The parent is overwhelmed by the degree of child emotional-behavioral problems and cannot develop an effective response to the child's emotional-behavioral issues.

☐ 17. **Family Context of Elevated Inter-Spousal Conflict**
Chronic child exposure to moderate-level inter-spousal conflict and anger or intermittent explosive episodes of highly angry inter-spousal conflict (intermittent spousal conflicts involving moderate anger that are successfully resolved are normal-range and are not elevated inter-spousal conflict).

Level 4: Positive Parenting

☐ 18. **Affectionate Involvement – Structured Spectrum**
Parenting includes frequent displays of parental affection and ***clearly structured*** rules and expectations for the child's behavior. Appropriate discipline follows from clearly defined and appropriate rules.

☐ 19. **Affectionate Involvement – Dialogue Spectrum**
Parenting includes frequent displays of parental affection and ***flexibly negotiated*** rules and expectations for the child's behavior. Parenting emphasizes dialogue, negotiation, and flexibility.

☐ 20. **Affectionate Involvement – Balanced**
Parenting includes frequent displays of parental affection and parenting effectively balances structured discipline with flexible parent-child dialogue.

Permissive to Authoritarian Dimension Rating: ________

0	10	20	30	40	50	60	70	80	90	100

Permissive Parenting	Flexible Dialogue Spectrum	Structured Discipline Spectrum	Authoritarian Parenting
Abusive Neglect: Extremely disengaged and neglectful parenting	Balanced Parenting		Hostile Abuse: Extremely hostile verbally and physically abusive parenting

← Normal Range Parenting →

Capacity for Authentic Empathy Rating:

1	2	3	4	5
Rigidly self-absorbed perspective; unable to de-center; absence of empathy	Tends to be rigidly self-absorbed; difficulty in de-centering and taking the perspective of others	Self-reflective; able to de-center from personal perspective to take the perspectives of others	Tends to be over-involved; diffusion of psychological boundaries between self-experience and child's experience	Enmeshed loss of psychological boundaries; projective identification of self-experience onto the child
Narcissistic Spectrum		Developmentally Healthy Range Empathy		Borderline Spectrum

Parental Issues of Clinical Concern (CC)

☐ CC 1: Parental schizophrenia spectrum issues

Stabilized on medication? ☐ Yes ☐ No ☐ Variable

☐ CC 2: Parental bipolar spectrum issues

Stabilized on medication? ☐ Yes ☐ No ☐ Variable

☐ CC 3: Parental major depression spectrum issues (including suicidality)

Stabilized by treatment? ☐ Yes ☐ No ☐ Variable

☐ CC 4: Parental substance abuse issues

Treated and in remission (1 yr)? ☐ Yes ☐ No ☐ Variable

☐ CC 5: Parental narcissistic or borderline personality disorder traits

In treatment? ☐ Yes ☐ No ☐ Variable

☐ CC 6: Parental history of trauma

Treated or in treatment? ☐ Yes ☐ No ☐ Variable

Appendix 6: Parent-Child Relationship Rating Scale

Parent-Child Relationship Rating Scale

Childress, C.A. (2015)

Date: ______________________________

Child's Name: ______________________ Parent's Name: ______________________

1. **Child Attitude: Hostile to Pleasant**

1	2	3	4	5	6	7
Openly hostile, mean, rude, disrespectful comments			Attitude is generally respectful. No openly hostile, mean, rude, or disrespectful comments. Child accepts displays of affection			Positive, warm, affectionate attitude. Child volunteers displays of affection.

2. **Child Cooperation: Behavioral Defiance to Cooperation**

1	2	3	4	5	6	7
Openly defiant of parental directives.			May complain and argue but is behaviorally compliant with parental directives within 2-3 additional prompts			Cooperative. Minimal to no argument.

3. **Child Sociability: Withdrawn to Social**

1	2	3	4	5	6	7
Withdrawn, sullen, non-communicative. Offers only one-word responses to questions			Is generally responsive to questions, offering elaborated responses. May become withdrawn when upset or angry.			Smiles easily and fairly often. Volunteers self-disclosures of his or her personal experiences.

4. **Parenting Style: Permissive to Structured**

1	2	3	4	5	6	7
Very lax and permissive. Little to no structure or discipline provided			Blend of behavioral expectations and discipline with negotiation and compromise			Highly structured, rule oriented, expectations for compliance and firm discipline.

Appendix 7: Outcome Questionnaires

AB-PA Key Intervention
Parent Satisfaction Questionnaire

Date:	

Parent's Name:	☐ mother ☐ father
Child's Name:	Child's Age:

1.) Prior to the AB-PA Key Intervention, I would rate my child's behavior toward me as:

1	2	3	4	5
Extremely bad & unacceptable		Moderately acceptable		Extremely good & fully acceptable

2.) Prior to the AB-PA Key Intervention, I would rate my child's behavior toward the other parent as:

1	2	3	4	5
Extremely bad & unacceptable		Moderately acceptable		Extremely good & fully acceptable

3.) My rating of my family's AB-PA therapist is:

1	2	3	4	5
Extremely bad & unacceptable		Moderately acceptable		Extremely good & fully acceptable

4.) My rating of my family's amicus attorney is:

1	2	3	4	5
Extremely bad & unacceptable		Moderately acceptable		Extremely good & fully acceptable

5.) My overall satisfaction with my family's involvement in the Key Intervention program is:

1	2	3	4	5
Extremely bad & unacceptable		Moderately acceptable		Extremely good & fully acceptable

AB-PA Key Intervention
AB-PA Therapist: Outcome Feedback Questionnaire

Date:	Therapist's Name:

Child's Name:	Child's Age:

Mother:	Father:

1. My rating of current family functioning is:

1	2	3	4	5
Extremely bad & unacceptable		Moderately acceptable		Extremely good & fully acceptable

2. My rating of the child's symptoms over the past 6 months is:

1	2	3	4	5
Extremely bad & unacceptable		Moderately acceptable		Extremely good & fully acceptable

3. My rating of the mother's insight and cooperation is:

1	2	3	4	5
Extremely bad & unacceptable		Moderately acceptable		Extremely good & fully acceptable

4. My rating of the father's insight and cooperation is:

1	2	3	4	5
Extremely bad & unacceptable		Moderately acceptable		Extremely good & fully acceptable

5. My overall rating of the family's progress toward treatment goals is:

1	2	3	4	5
Extremely bad & unacceptable		Moderately acceptable		Extremely good & fully acceptable

6. My rating of the amicus attorney (name:______________________________) is:

1	2	3	4	5
Extremely bad & unacceptable		Moderately acceptable		Extremely good & fully acceptable

AB-PA Key Intervention
Amicus Attorney: Outcome Feedback Questionnaire

Date:	Therapist's Name:

Child's Name:	Child's Age:

Mother:	Father:

1. My rating of current family functioning is:

1	2	3	4	5
Extremely bad & unacceptable		Moderately acceptable		Extremely good & fully acceptable

2. My rating of the child's symptoms over the past 6 months is:

1	2	3	4	5
Extremely bad & unacceptable		Moderately acceptable		Extremely good & fully acceptable

3. My rating of the mother's insight and cooperation is:

1	2	3	4	5
Extremely bad & unacceptable		Moderately acceptable		Extremely good & fully acceptable

4. My rating of the father's insight and cooperation is:

1	2	3	4	5
Extremely bad & unacceptable		Moderately acceptable		Extremely good & fully acceptable

5. My overall rating of the family's progress toward treatment goals is:

1	2	3	4	5
Extremely bad & unacceptable		Moderately acceptable		Extremely good & fully acceptable

7. My rating of the AB-PA therapist (name:______________________________) is:

1	2	3	4	5
Extremely bad & unacceptable		Moderately acceptable		Extremely good & fully acceptable

ABOUT THE AUTHOR

Dr. Childress is a licensed clinical psychologist currently in private practice in Claremont, California. He is the author of An Attachment-Based Model of Parental Alienation: Foundations, and The Narcissistic Parent: A Guidebook for Legal Professionals Working with Families in High-Conflict Divorce. Prior to entering private practice, Dr. Childress served as the Clinical Director for children's assessment and treatment center, primarily working with children in the foster care system. The clinical focus of Dr. Childress is child and family therapy, the treatment of Attention Deficit Hyperactivity Disorder (ADHD), angry and oppositional children, parent-child conflicts, parenting, and marital problems, and he has an additional clinical expertise in early childhood mental health, with a focus on attachment-related pathologies and the neurodevelopment of the brain during childhood.

Made in the USA
Monee, IL
05 November 2026

67375660R00031